Hope Blossoming

in their Ink

Hope

blossoming

in their ink

Juan Garrido-Salgado

PUNCHER & WATTMANN

First published in 2020
Published by Puncher and Wattmann
PO Box 279
Waratah NSW 2298

http://www.puncherandwattmann.com
puncherandwattmann@bigpond.com

NATIONAL
LIBRARY
OF AUSTRALIA

A catalogue entry for this book is available from the National Library of Australia.

ISBN   9781925780703

Cover design by Miranda Douglas

Printed by Lightning Source International

Contents

Part 1: I was Here I was There

Part 2: Australia Remains Far Away

Part 3: Poems of Struggle & Revolution

Part 1:
I was Here I was There

'Some truths are so near and obvious to the mind that a man need only open his eyes
to see them.'
— Jorge Luis Borges, *A New Refutation of Time*

Talking with Nicanor Parra in Santiago in 1981

Young poets/say whatever you want.
Pick your own style/much blood has gone under the bridge
To still believe - I believe/that there's only one way to cross the road:
You can do anything in poetry.
— *Nicanor Parra*

I remember
When we arrived at your home in *la Reina*.
The dogs barking at us.
After a few minutes you appeared
Like a ghost in the afternoon.
Mr *Anti-poeta*.
I was born in the Barros Lucos Hospital.
I never went to the University.
However, I swing between two oceans.
I translate poetry in English into Spanish,
As a creative pathway (*puente*)
Between two different cultures and lands.
Here I am
Listening to a Chinese-Australian poet
Listening to an Iraqi poet
Listening to Aboriginal poets
Reading with my mind Australian poetry.

I agree with you
The style doesn't come from a creative writing course.
My style comes from reading other poets, from passion
and learning the rhythm of the bird in a tree.
Learning how to plant seeds; preparing the plot, watering,
Looking after them every day.
I agree again with you
Mr when you say
Much blood has gone under the bridge.

Most of my poets are dead. Some of them
Have been killed or have suicided.
Essenin, Roque Dalton, Neruda, Vallejo.
Only Huidobro was a poet of the bourgeois-revolution.
Ernesto Cardenal survived the Pope's sin against the Revolution
as well as the collapse of the Sandinista revolution.
So they killed the poets amongst the struggling people.
I have been on the path of the struggle, in prison,
Tortured by the Chilean secret police.
When I went to your home
You welcomed us.
In this time I was an invisible poet with a few poems in my heart.
Victor Hugo Romo talked to you.
You showed us your rooms,
frames on the walls with newspaper headlines,
as great paintings.
Your cat was like a prince in the poet's palace.
You were happy to read your poems at the concert
That we organised in tribute to Violeta Parra.

After more than twenty years
I am sure you remember me very well
If I say my name to you:

I am Juan
My nickname was el Negro.
I worked in Nuestro Canto's office 1980
With Miguel Dagvanino and John Smith.
I wrote a book
Variantes de la Libertad Definitiva
By Samuel Lafferte,
Published by Hondero Entusiasta Press.

Yes I remember you very well.
Your house
With pictures from newspapers on the walls
Replacing the paintings of Picasso, Miro or Dali.
By the way
Could you tell me how to find the way out of this conversation?

Nicanor Parra says:
You can do anything in poetry.
You can do anything in poetry.
You can
do anything
in
poetry.

Reading Milozs's story about happiness

Milozs remembers being a boy of ten living on the farm
Of his grandparents in Lithuania.
Happiness experienced in childhood does not pass
Without a trace: the memory of ecstasy dwells in our body
And possesses a strong curative power.

I'm back in my
Ten year old boyhood
Knocking on the old wooden door with the steel handle.
I touch the grimy old hand; it's greeting me from many years past
But I am an unmoving figure there, waiting for a word
Or a neighbour to respond to my quest.

I hear the voice of a boy; I put my left ear closer to the door.
Yes! I recognise it. It is my twin brother, Carlos.
He shouts from the patio at the end of the long corridor.
Weeds, roses, daisies, trees
Grapes and wine, all those still a part of life.
Wait a minute! he replies, among the mad barking of dogs.

It's not Carlos. An old man appears
His face a silhouette at the back door...Don Emilio.
He invites me in for a cup of tea.
The kitchen still has an image in my memory.
His words are like
A home-made film with a white sheet in a dark room
Showing us how much we enjoyed living there.

Carlos and I stay there at the bus stop
Like two sailors waiting for a ship arriving into port.
When we see our *Abuela*, we smile to her as a handkerchief to the air.
She kisses us and we walk home together.
She always brought food and gifts as eternal presents.
When she arrived I never needed yesterday to kick the ball all morning.
When she arrived I never needed tomorrow to play any games.

My mobile rings! A voice I don't recognise asks me,
What time will you be back home?
I lived without yesterday or tomorrow, in the eternal present...

Monday 12 July at 2 pm

I can't think about your anniversary.
At 2 pm, I don't want to be here:
A coffee shop next to the entry of
Woolworths Shopping Centre at Hilton.
I try to write a poem for you, Viejo Neruda
But prices & offers tangle up my hands;
I'm trapped by products.

I drink my long black & see
    Shelf Prices Reduced
    In Green
1–10 long & narrow corridors.
In the street the wind battles with clouds
And rain wounds the pavement.
It is cold, my bike is an old poem
Leaning against a line of shopping trolleys
Like an old figure's head in the middle of nowhere
Como un viejo mascarón de proa en el medio de ningún lugar.

Your voice came from this verse:
Venid a ver la sangre por las calles.
I can still recite this poem by heart.

G'day mate, someone said to me;
He carries a green bag.
I drink my long black
& I can see Special Price: Kellogg's Cereal. Any 2 for $9.00
I can see Special Price: Huggies Nappies. Any 2 for $32.00

Noise is traffic junk in the car park, shopping trolleys.
Customers want to leave soon and go home.
Your voice is still in my head & your verses in my mouth.
I can't shut up; your verses come out louder,
Like a strong wind shaking the remaining leaves
Of the gum tree in the corner of the car park.
I can't shut up; your verses come out louder.

Venid a ver la sangre por las calles.
Venid a ver
La sangre por las calles.

I meet with a yubba in an old secondhand bookshop at Grote Street

Friday 20th, this month of Autumn in my city, after work,
Instead of going to the pub I went to a second-hand bookshop in Grote
  Street.
In the quiet, I sweated and watched the sunset forgetful of other tasks.
Near the end of my search I thought I saw from a lot of books on the
  shelf
Books that were marked as Aboriginal.
Yoogum Yoogum, by Lionel Fogarty, Penguin books. 1982.

I leafed through the pages of each poem quickly
I saw names, verses and time, September 1982.
Words came to my eyes as if I was walking through a long tunnel.
With my heart wounded I flew back to that year in one of the pages:
Yoogum Yoogum.

I read the deep anger and hurt of many generations of totally oppressed
Black Australians, said Gary Foley.

With those words, I landed on the roof of my old home.
It was a raid on every house in the city by the secret police.
I was already a poet with a bunch of poems surviving
the fire of oppression and many books were buried
in a huge hole on the patio.
Before I came back from my trip to USSR, 1982.

Yoogum Yoogum
I read the poem, by Lionel.
I am tired of writing.
Where I can hear his rhythm of freedom
Painless are my words.

July 1982 had my own wounds and resistance lines.
Barricades incomplete, political dreams underground.
taking hours off a duty to continue fighting until victory.

Yoogum Yoogum
Books that were buried years as seed resistance
Poetry is a flag rising upwind of freedom in people's hearts.
Poems the pathway of freedom fighters: Lionel Fogarty and Samuel
  Lafferte.

Yoogum Yoogum
Hasta la Victoria Siempre
Yubba poet

Tango for Domingo Cerda Cruz

1

Y yo me hice el Tango
I make myself into a tango
listening
to melodies of passion,
movements/bodies
dance
in the naked night
where shadows in the corridor move
rhythm with memories and tears.
The past
asks him
sharp questions
here on the dance floor
in the mirror of his eyes.

I dance
I kiss not for love
only for life
that dances
in the last train of my age.

I remember him in the railway station of a non-country.
He wears a cloudy hat for his last trip.
It is midnight
in the suitcase and black umbrella of 1963.
I chew the absence of bread and milk
by the table and bed of my own life.

Here on the dance-floor
in the mirror of her eyes
he makes himself into a tango,
dances and drinks of wine and love
to forget the last rotten kiss
she gave him in the *último poema del desamor*.

2

Tango del abuelo
Tango for my grandfather.
He sits there
in the corner of our old house.
He converses with the tiredness of years
in a bottle of red
hidden somewhere in the kitchen.
The wine embraces him
within melodies of the *bandoneón*.
Outside, the moon moves slowly in the distant mirror;
stars dance for him.
He drinks the solitude of the dusk of July 1990.
The night is the tyranny of his failures
kissing his dried memories of death.
I look through the window
my key a ghost going into the lock of his own sadness.

3

Domingo Cerda Cruz
He died in 1991, Santiago.
His funeral:
my visa of long solitary confinement.
Yes! I arrived in Australia
with a humanitarian visa in 1990
according to the Immigration laws

you have to be at least 2 years
in the country without leaving.
Military Law
gave me only three months to leave Chile.

Y yo me hice el Tango
    Death
    Distance
    Dislocation
Tristeza. Muerte. Distancia. Dislocación.
My passport became
A prison or funeral
For my dear father-grandfather.
I say goodbye to him
within the mirror of my own past
with a candle and red carnation
I listen to his favourite tango.

Y yo me hice el Tango
Porque el tango es macho
Porque el tango es fuerte
Tiene olor a vida y tiene gusto a muerte.

4

I remember his tango; I am the son of Domingo Cerda Cruz
My blood is a dry river in his native dream.
Now his absence in your heart
is like a move to another country.
Language is a desert   on your lips
Language is an oasis   in your heart
Years of mirage.
Words are dying birds
nesting in your broken tongue.
Again you are in an exile

of the blank paper of non-existence.
Invisible *vuelos* arrive into Sydney airport your adopted land.

Y yo me hice el Tango.

5

Please, *levántate*
and dance with me, *viejo querido,*
dance with your whole body of love.
It can be a *bandoneón*
where death and life
kiss your mask and embrace you and her
as one rhythm of passion,
movement of reality and misery.
Oh! *Bandoneón!*
Let him play the rhythm of death or revolution,
kiss his hungry body.
Listen *bandoneón*
my tears *cayendo* in the dreams
of coldness that killed
his heart in April,
when he left this land of blank paper.

Please, *levántate,*
dance with me
this night of melody, life, love and tango.
Please, *levántate,*
dance with me, *viejo querido,*
kiss me with distance and oblivion
on this open wound of my heart again and again,
donde nacerán vuelos para vivir en tu distancia
donde vivirán los vuelos del recuerdo en la memoria.

Javier Chavez's Sunflowers

On the 30th anniversary of the fascist coup in Chile

It was September.
After his talk in the Semaphore Workers Club
Javier planted sunflowers in Aunty Veronica's plot.
The holes were like rivers of memory
That embrace us with earth.
Silence and distance grow there.
I looked after them
When Javier retuned to Chile.

Now I am watering them with friendship.
Soon they will be sun with roots on earth
giving memory to my eyes and heart in the afternoon.

November is the month that I will write a letter to Javier.
It will make our friendship flourish more than ever.

Today, there will be ten suns in the garden
Like yellow wings playing with the breeze,
Heads of life and struggle that will not fly away
Either to the sea, or to the sky
Either to the mountain, or to the desert.

Because they were born to live in the garden of friendship.
Because they were born to be a memory and light.

When terror was a dark flower in my country
When terror nested in every tree of fear in my country
Javier Chavez was one of those who always sowed
Seeds of hope and resistance in the underground
In the blood and terror of our bodies and land.
Today, there will be ten suns in the garden

Like yellow wings playing with the breeze.
We planted them together like a friendship
For those who fight for a revolution on earth.

Tattoo on a night of five Moons

November 25th 1985.
My other words said
They were drawing on my skin.
It was an invisible drawing of terror.
Days, hours in the afternoon
Where secret police (CNI) stripped me
Naked and drew a race of wild horses on me.
Blood and sweat were spilt
By galloping furious hooves
Into my flesh and dreams forever.

It was dark, my heart barking as a wounded dog
Licking a night of five Moons.
Lamiendo una noche de cinco lunas.

Now my other tongue
Sang like a sparrow
On the threshold of your window's dream.

Today

Today I live on death row.
I am the one who mumbles in the cold air that goes through here.
I am the one who lies down and relives;
Who is covered with foliage rustling silence,
Who speaks of remembrance in the darkness of the walls.
Clean stones, blown leaves scratch your name
And I sit in the trunk of tranquillity.
I sink to death with this question: what am I doing here
All night long without understanding what makes my life bleed?

Wounded Wings

I am a shadow that embraces something.
I am not flying over, anymore.
Thursday I am tired and I've lost the ability to enjoy myself.
(My) wound is beyond the body and soul.
(Self) is silence and where I live has only four walls.
I am the one who stole those wings
And put them on.
Now it's too late to return them.
I am responsible.
I lick my wounded wings
Silence.

I am a citizen waiting for

I consume anything if it is cheap
I don't read & I don't pray
I work as a horse in the dry field.
Instead of eating hay I eat time for money.
I don't drink from the bank of illusion.
I prefer a few beers at happy hour.
A gum tree is the only inhabitant in my home
As an intruder or an old dream in my front window
I have fucking nothing else.

I am a refugee of long hours

Time is a wound in my soul.
A dream sank in the distance between us.

It is now a revolution.
A mobile phone
Off
Within my own flesh.

Last night

My heart a wreck
With a drunk crew
One by one
Sinking to the bottom.

Only my eyes survive.
I look
On the hull.
Hundreds of pirates offer me a tequila jar
To celebrate the new adventure.

A storm is coming.
I survive.

In the distance, the sky's mirror winks.

After seven days of hot weather

He makes a confession
In front of a glass of cold beer.
It is another hot day.
The mirror has its own reflection
Of all sins.

In a few seconds
The word is not
Belching pain in the bottom of the cup.
'I am a sinner', he said

The confessional is closed.
Everyone has left the bar.
On the street
I devour the night
Like an invisible dog
Barking at my own soul.

Talking to my granddaughter

I prepare a fire
In the living room
On a cold night in May.

Nene-oudou one year old
Crawls and stands up
At the coffee table
As a barricade against
Les Miserables by Victor Hugo,
The book's cover hot in her hand.

Her body is alert to the danger
Or perhaps the flames
Are stranger symbols of life
For her fire is creation.
For her it looks like a new life
Nene-oudou sees a new life.
And listens to my words in Spanish.
I warn her of danger
That is close.
And she responds in her words,
A mixed inheritance by birth
(French, Liberian, Spanish and English).
The sounds from her lips are clear:
Rghoo gaoo tata hooo whoo.

We dance the ancient rhythms
Of laughter & love.
She understands I think.
The danger of the fire is in her eyes.

'Go to be lost to others, overwhelmed by bones and light and themselves'

Inspired by John Kinsella's 'The Merry-Go-Round by the Sea' a Randolph Stow novel

There are lights that will never burn out
Until they make bodies and dust
In our hearts and hands.
>*Hay luces que no sé apagaran jamás*
>*Hasta que lleguen hacer cuerpos y polvo*

En nuestros corazones y manos.
And history is written in letters clear and simple.
For those generations of oblivion
Again see the light in the bones of those who disappeared.

>*Y la historia se escriba con letras clara y simple.*
>*Para que esas generaciones del olvido*
>*Vuelvan a ver la luz en los huesos de los que desaparecieron.*

Of those who were buried, tortured and crushed
No compassion in the brutality of Contreras, Pinochet
And 1,500 agents of DINA-CNI.
>*De esos que fueron enterrados, torturados y machacados*
>*Sin compasión por la brutalidad de los Contreras, Pinochet*
>*y los 1.500 agentes de la Dina-CNI.*

I take these verses from John Kinsella.
I squeeze out light, dusted with the bones of my yesterday.
I go into the forest of absence.
I walk among trees of distance and pain.
>*Tomó estos versos de John Kinsella*
>*Los estrujo de luz, los desempolvo de huesos de mi ayer.*
>*Me adentro en el bosque de la ausencia*
>*Camino entre los árboles de la distancia y el dolor.*

Later in the foliage I saw a bird
Nibbling light on a leaf falling to the ground.
I said, they are the life that is returning
To plant dreams in the forest of memory.

Luego entre el follaje vi un pájaro
picoteando la luz en una hoja cayendo a la tierra
me dije, son ellos es la vida que vuelve
a sembrar sueños en el bosque de la memoria.

Back in Santiago they call it
Peace Park, Villa Grimaldi, the former home of torture.
It seems that only yesterday there were cries of torture and death.
Yes, long ago I walked among roses,
Walls of their names and tributes from many traces of evil.

Allá en Santiago le llaman:
Parque por la Paz, de Villa Grimaldi.
Parece que solo ayer fue gritos de tortura y muerte.
Sí, anduve tiempo atrás entre rosas,
muros de sus nombres y tributos entre tantas huellas de la maldad.

There I fell into tears and I knew that poetry
Still continues to be torn apart by humanity.

Ahí caí en llanto y supe que la poesía
Aún se sigue desgarrando por la humanidad.

Koolunga: Poetry Night was a gift of the spirit

For Ali Cobby-Eckermann and Lionel Fogarty

Miles that are drawing us
Closer to the poetry.

We met after leaving
We rode as if the sunset was just waiting
Behind the memories and traces of what we are.

The memory it opens
Is like a dry leaf from a tree in the middle of nowhere.
The unknown leads us to the pastures of the dusk.
Silence is a bird that knows nothing of strangers.
Wind blows uncertainly, lying quietly, not fresh.

Towards the left side of the trail a sign: two churches and a pub
After a long plain we enter the town of the poets...
Friendship invites voices, papers and words to celebrate.
Koolunga where the word comes from the earth.
Koolunga where the spirit builds its home.

Ali and Lionel are poets who are awakening the forest.
Ali and Lionel write the dawn of Koolunga,
Guide the crafting of fresh verses,
Words with the sounds of birds, shrivelled desert rivers
& share the food of creation.
Poetry Night was a gift of the spirit.

Playing chess against a maldita white queen

In this game each of us has 1 King, 1 Queen, 2 Rooks, 2 Bishops, 2 Knights and 8 Pawns
on 64 squares

I
The board is an interesting battlefield.
I am ready to start; I don't know about you.
I don't see you there on the other side of the abyss,
I don't remember playing with you before.
Who are you, maldita white queen?
Where are your strategies and tactics?
Is it the French defence?
Because the French defence gives up control
Of the centre of the board to the white.

It feels as if my pieces have been paralysed in your territory.
I have to think more about the Ruy Lopez, Opening Tactics (1561),
And how to develop his tactics in my game.

II
My attack is to occupy your territory
& if possible to create my kingdom in your heart,
To write into your flesh a Chinese horse's verse,
Or a Mayan prayer for humanity.
That will be my best defence against your attack.
I can also sacrifice my pieces and their positions
To create more space for balance and harmony in our game.

III
My black pieces move there & over there on the board
(It feels as if I am playing a five-minute game).
I am tired and disconcerted without tactics,
Losing my pieces in this game.
My pawns struggle to create a good defence

Moving with difficulty & doubt.
I am a king without land with a wounded heart
Dying within your territory of indifference.
In the abyss of the board I pause as a horse rider
Thinking deeply about the next move.
I am surrounded by remoteness and flames.
Death is the next and definite move.
I am dying with the tears of loneliness
& the victory of your checkmate.

Before I slept

Y deshojar la rosa de los pesares
Bajo la indiferencia de otro sol y otro cielo
— *Nicolás Guillén*

The bohemian at home dresses up as a ghost.
He drinks and talks around the four empty chairs.
He has a dark scowl.
He has a drink of Cuban rum with coke
                    (even if he hates this drink).

To open the gate of exile is painful.
He shuts his eyes as a full moon
Incites him to touch the gentle blue of the candy flesh of a youth.

Eight minutes for a poem

Sitting next to my first cup of coffee
I don't know which direction to take.
The taste & black sea
Warm swims & the dawn
Inside my soul swim as a fish in the deep ocean.
Memory is crashed
Wounds & blood are moans for life.
Breath is the earth into the water.

Breath is a last minute word or thought – nothing else.

Before & After 8.30am

So many things to do: take a shower
Prepare yourself for the day.
Bed is a ship arriving at the port window.
I open the curtain like putting down the ship's sails.
Wash last night's dishes
As if talking with many friends.

I am tired.
A pen & blank paper
I draw a line.

The alarm of my mobile sounds again:
You have to pick up Gordon at the garden at 8.10 am

Variations on moments of silence

1

Entro a mi mente como un pájaro a su jaula al atardecer.
I enter my mind like a bird entering a cage at dawn.

2

En mi mano sostengo una taza de té de Van Gogh.
Entro a su cama como un color de la agonía en el silencio.
In my hand I hold a Van Gogh cup of tea.
I am going into his bedroom with the colour of agony's silence.

3

I read a verse from Borges; darkness is a rhythm of the moon
dropping two blind stars into the poem. Silence is born in my dream.

4

I am a poet eating the silence between the walls and my open wounds.
In my prison cell 1987 silence is the only river to swing away my pain.

A yellow leaf is falling from a peach tree

It's a yellow gift in my hand
A yellow and long leaf
Falling in an April afternoon near my notebook.
I catch it.

With my brush-ink
I draw its broken wing.

It's a dried yellow tear falling from an old branch in April.

It's a yellow vowel in the language of the autumn.
A yellow drop is falling to the gutter.
A yellow feather of a wounded bird that spent the night
talking to the shadow of the peach tree.

It's a yellow gift for my eyes
Dressed up as a butterfly lost in the autumn of my poem.

I made the bed at midnight

Shake the clean sheets
as a goodbye handkerchief.
They lie in your shadow, where you left
again I shake the second to stretch it;
from below come thousands of dead wings as a last flight;
where the mattress claims your absence.

I made the bed with clean sheets,
blankets stretched...
The quilt wrinkles my body like a southern poncho
crushes me, suffocating me in the abandoned
and you pull the door as if you wrinkle a piece of paper.
They are rubble that falls on the road.

Life: toss me a coin

Vida: tírame una moneda

Why do I have to write this poem? I don't want to do it.

I would like to go outside and get lost in the noise of the street.

I would like just to be able to walk
Like that man with sunglasses carrying a plastic bag of fruit.

I could follow him, tell him where the sun is, or peel an orange
at his table and have a conversation on life. No, perhaps

I could go out and walk next to a beautiful blonde woman in a black
   dress,
and high heel shoes and take her for a walk to dry her tears.

However she is not a widow. She just loves black like anyone in the
   office.
Why do I have to write this poem?

I smile at a person from my table and it seems to be reflected in a mirror.
I fly like a bird through a long tunnel
Trying to catch the smile as my only meal of the day.

End of July, 2011

Waiting for a poem:
It has to be a painful process.
I am here sitting at my desk
Waiting for hours but nothing comes through.
I push and push like a pregnant woman.
I can see spots of blood on the page.

I ring the doctor and ask him, what can I do?
I feel like I have been waiting for nine months already,
but the poem is not born.
I can't walk, sleep, breathe anymore.
The doctor asks me: are you a poet?

I am already late for work.
I wake up, but my dream was (or is?) trapped in another body.

A dialogue with myself

I know rain. I see meaning.
Touch it and drink.
— Stephen Lawrence

I'm reading Huxley's *Brave New World* (*Mundo Feliz*)
at Lucia's.
So what have I written today?
...I don't know...Perhaps.

How much rain has been in our city?
24 hours of rain to 9 am —
25 mm to 49 mm.
Cloudy-light winds — Adelaide Area.
And I remember
In Adelaide
A poet died last week.
I met Stephen Lawrence
A poet who applauded my verses without translation;
A poet who shared a brief evening in the tent of the Adelaide Writers'
    Week 2012.
I don't know
yo no sé
I don't know
        yo no sé
In Adelaide a poet died last week.
Stephen Lawrence wrote his last verses.
Stephen Lawrence left us next to our blank page
Pages we have to fill with silence, our lament of emptiness
Rays of light that are slowly bringing us life.

A rose bush blossomed as a poet died

For Gonzalo Rojas

Filled with winter and the beauty of Lebu
it gave us roses with deep roots in the flesh,
in laughter and love.
He sang, loved and cultivated his garden with dark hands.

I read him, heard him read his poems
with his voice like freshly fallen petals of sweat
caressing naked skin.
I saw him there in Mapocho Station
as the trains arrived from his reading filled with journeys,
cars filled with people and applause.
In each poem we were travellers on unique journeys.
Our hearts fell into the ocean of his carnal rose bush.

A rose bush blossomed as the poet Gonzalo Rojas died.
I demand an autopsy to read the verses trapped
in death or the silence of the cold gaze of goodbyes.
What did he write in death's finality?
What did his eyes say to us, clawing the white walls of hope?
Where did he hide those last lines written
between wounded brain and the heart that is dying?
Who will translate for us into death's language
or the language of eternal life
the last lines the poet spoke?

I will visit the roses of his eternal garden in Lebu.
I will visit the place I love,
there between the street's daily comings and goings,
this old paradise God gave to him.

Conversation with Yahia Al-Samawy

I

Before her departure,
I was a living person
Sentenced to death
— Yahia Al-Samawy's 'A Tombstone from the Marble of Words'

Crossing the bridge made by bones & howls,
words & ancient stories of struggles.
We share a poetry reading for peace.
Our spirits are survivors
from masses of hard, very hard blows.

César Vallejo the Peruvian poet wrote:
Hay golpes en la vida, tan fuerte…yo no sé

There are blows in life so hard…I don't know.
We share from that mass of hard, very hard blows
that broke our bones, dug hatred into our flesh.
After they laughed and ordered us to drink blood or urine
blindfolds came to our eyes like wings tumbling through the air
their hands enormous fly swatters on our heads.

But our birds remain alive
fluttering from our souls into the world.

We choose, Yahia and I, to struggle *hasta vencer.*
Our talk doesn't fluently speak of the wounds in English syllables
but gives us the opportunity to share death and life.

He flew from the hell of darkness, survived in prison
as an Arabic long poem.
His mother's death is a seed planted in his blank moon.

My grandpa died.
At his funeral I was only a fragment of the poem inside his heart.

Exile is a long road. Yahia's reading is a howl for humanity,
his verse a mirror of sand and footprints where silence is captive.
In Australia our soldiers still kill in the name of democracy.

II

'Now I have one more reason
Not to betray my country…'

Words sound like the open ears of a fresh artichoke
grown to eat at the table of beauty and pain.

We remember. They left us in tears, howls of torture
still echoing in our memories and verse.

In his country his name
could not be spoken,
even at the side of his dying mother's bed.

In his home in Baghdad
each syllable of his poems a dagger, blood
or torture for somebody.

Su prisión con dientes sangrando en las encías del odio,
uñas decapitadas con cuchillos del mal.
En la prisión de aislamiento fui sombra bebiéndose la oscuridad,
el dolor y la pasión.

Bars and darkness live in the city of Baghdad and Santiago's 1973.
Books, papers, libraries are ashes of horror and fire.
Words were persecuted like acts of betrayal against humanity

Death, death his mother dying without her son.
A shadow walked close to the coffin that morning.

III

'After her departure,
I became a dead person
Sentenced to life.'

Reading at Monsalvat.
Headline: Writers Disturbing the Peace.
What peace are we talking about?
The intervention on Aboriginal lands?
The Peace that accepted the occupied territory in Palestine?
The Peace that killed thousands of Timorese
and destroyed their land and homes?

The Peace that ruined centuries of Baghdad's history?
The Peace that burned books in the streets of Santiago, Chile, 1973?

We were both political prisoners.
Both countries were sentenced to death
by Richard Nixon in 1973
& G.W. Bush in 2008.

The world sleeps now and doesn't remember those tragedies.
We still write for peace to honour our martyrs and people in the struggle.

At home, in our Adelaide garden
The roses have names: Salvador Allende,
Victor, Gladys, Gerardo and Javier.
These roses talk to us and give us courage
as well as the smell of beauty.

Memory is food for the struggle. *Hasta Vencer.*

I feel blessed today

I try to get inspired reading Shakespeare (*A Brief Insight*, by G. Greer)
When I sit down to write a poem.
It was a heavy door to open and it made a noise like an old inhabitant of
the house.
I put the book away.
My heart sleeps, my eyes fluttering around wings
Knocking on the window.
I was in Moore Crafts shop (Monday).
Few people looked at the beautiful handmade things.
I was finishing a line of an uncompleted poem
When a small Aboriginal woman passing through
Smiled at me
And disappeared in the tunnel of business.
Was she a spirit? Or an old citizen of this ancient land?
I know, an Aboriginal woman walked into this poem.
Can you feel it?

Part 2:
Australia Remains Far Away

'Yeah, every poet needs a place to call home
Every poet needs a place to call home'

— Samuel Wagan Watson, *Love Poems and Death Threats*

The war remains far away

Bullets are images & sounds
Crashing into the TV room.

Humanity is Wilde's Selfish Giant.
Prayer is unfashionable.
War remains far away.
Our response is silent & distant
As if an invisible soldier is assaulting our breath.

We tick yes or no.
Everything is like a shopping list of our needs for the week.
And our relationships become takeaway meals.

Australia 2005

My verses are like vessels navigating two oceans.
Waves are words speaking on the shore of any pub
Drinking the solitude of the inner ocean
And drawing it into my eyes.
The horizon of verses that stretches across heart space.
In this new land, I buy vegetables at the Central Market.
I read a few novels and poetry books.
I dig the soil and plant seeds to grow as hope in this land.

My other ocean is always a paper boat.
Verse and spirit are my reading:
Cortázar, Neruda, Vallejo, Vicente Huidobro,
And Ernesto Cardenal, an old poet from *la revolución de Nicaragua*.
The scars are still there, an ancient road in the south of my land.
They dwell within death, hope blossoming in their ink.

Invasion Day, 2012

For Ali Cobby Eckermann & Lionel Fogarty

I slept last night within your kiss and I woke up invaded by a stroking
    hand.
In our patio last night Ali & Lionel talked about dreams and reality;
Conversation of spirit and friends who find they are united by love and
    dignity.
We are expatriate voices
Tortured birds that write poems for liberation.
Lionel writes verses against terra nullius
& Ali has kissed the flesh of her sister who flew above the earth.
Juan is still reading his poem 'I look like an Aboriginal'.
Around the table the candles light our faces and the wind plays with the
    flames.
Our bodies are embracing the smoke of words & tongues tangling
With accents of life & exile.
We are surviving the words & accents of struggle and resistance;
The sound of English is not a celebration.
We are birds trapped in the broken branches of flesh of the ancestors'
    sorrow.
Here we are. Together in unity within a night away from the invasion
    day.
Candles illuminate the accent of our laughter.
The smoke is lost through the sky. We laugh. We are warriors and poets.
We are brothers and sisters in this invaded land.
We are pulling out the Mayan calendar sheet 2012.
We are going to die and be born again in our common struggle for
    freedom.

In the Pub (Scene of the Last Resurrection)

Silence is a thirst on the edge of an imaginable ocean.
You appear at the door.
We drink at the shore like sailors on a hot day.

We drink and talk about religion.
Behind us the moon is an old lamp
Of the Russian poet Serguei Esenin.
Paradise is not up there, I say, it's here on earth.
Your red dress is the flesh of the rose petals in my garden.
Outside, a stranger knocks, wind of a drunken dusk.

Thank God it's Friday.
A sin rests in my mind.
I drink a cold beer and bite a red apple
in the paradise of our conversation.

Thank God it's Friday.
As we leave the pub
I glimpse the Dalai Lama
And the smile of Ho Chi Minh on the wall near the bar.

Both give me a wink to cheer my last resurrection.
In the streets of an empty town
I ride like an angel returning from the tomb.

Red Chilli

A long and narrow fruit
Red and hot without water or wine
You can't eat.
A volcano grows in you
Where the lava invades your eyes and tongue
And you are lost for words.
Chilli is *muy picante.*

You feel naked inside a dry river
Surrounded by
Thousands of wild horses in your heart
Truena, arde y devora todo.
I eat chilli in the garden
I drink water from the mountain
As seagulls survive
On the shore of the red sea.

Summer's morning about 11am

In the garden.
Why?
         Why?
Rex is drinking the blood and flesh
Of the bird.
He eats
feathers and bones
as his meal of the day.

I stand
invisible witness
watching him.

I touch my wounded wings.
The dog
ate
my brother.

Cultural Difference

I like drinking *mate* in the afternoon or at night.

However, I have to drink it
Only from memory or with my ghost friend
Around the table by the fire.

Mate, a hot drink of herbs
Prepared by boiling *la tetera*
The bulb crushed in a bowl.
There is great conversation with *mate.*

What are the effects of *mate*, mate?

Apart from a great time, if you drink too much
You have to spend the whole night
Trying to write new poems by the light of an angry moon
Or praying
So that he can give you some time to sleep.

Poetry Reading at Aldinga Beach

Vowels come and go from you Darío
Your blue poem.
Some twenty seagulls
Stand nearby on one foot
Sharing your words.
Windy, indeed.
The wind runs over the waves
Jumping through (and appearing far) in the tranquil blue.

Waves just touch the shore
An invisible track where we were reading the blue.

A car roars a huge sound
Not a monster from the sea.
Seagulls fly in a flash
Wind and wings applauding far into the air.
You Dario, at Aldinga Beach.

Love is a dead butterfly

The body of a dead butterfly;
I am the one who buries her flesh.

I close the door with my wounded wings.
Have a good night, I say.
In my dream roses eat your body.

Afternoon at the hairdresser

A little boy, blond and straight hair
Two years old, blue eyes.
He sits in the barber's chair.
His mum says,
'He will be two years old tomorrow'.

I wait my turn looking in the mirror at an old memory.
I am sitting in front of a screen waiting for the film to start.
My son is two years & I'm taking him to the barber for the first time.
He is an old customer 'knowing what to do'.
His mum says to him, 'Look in the mirror'.
For me it is like an old movie 17 years ago,
I enjoy remembering.
I laugh with the little boy as if I smile with my son.
The film is finished. It is my turn.
The little boy says goodbye to us. I say, 'Happy Birthday'.

My barber says to me later, 'I feel sick, my back is so weak when I bend,
Broken and painful.
I can't cut kids' hair anymore.
It is too difficult; any movement from kids is a storm.'

I feel like a ghost with sharp scissors in my hands.

I was talking to a spider last night

1

She was making her nest in darkness.
I lit a candle.
The flames and thread gave me a simple life.
A huge cloud of smoke covered her body.
I thought, she is moving away.
Instead, the spider talked to me,
The wind became a huge hand of hot air
That beat me on my face.
I felt it was the end of the conversation
& started a war until one of us died.

2

She came back on one of the walls of the kitchen;
I mean the spider
Walking through the south-east side of the window frame.
Her name is Juanita. She worked hard. She made something,
Cleaned her clothes & fed her babies.
I was there watching everything on the threshold of the night.

3

This morning I had breakfast. I couldn't wait to see her again.
Perhaps, she will soon go forever.
She appeared as a humble creature in one of the corners.
I said, 'Can we talk without fighting?'
She said, 'Yes'.
And a language began to exist between us.

The Cow in the field at Mayfield

1

Far away in a field a cow moves
As she ruminates on her own cud.
The wind will herd clouds
To the east where the hills
Wait to drink the rain of the afternoon.

2

There is a black crow
Making a sound in the distance.
Between you and me
A bird is flapping in the open space
Of immensity.

3

I am sitting on this land
Surrounded by hills, grasslands,
Animals, birds and gum trees.
I think: am I sitting here in my Tata's dream?
Am I harvesting the vegetables of my childhood?
Over there the cow is eating the setting moon.

4

Who am I in this afternoon?
A red rain of blood, a sweet rain
Or simply a spit of wind
In a drunken cloud of distance and solitude.

5

Perhaps I am a cloud
Over a hill
A carriage made from an old tree
With two galloping kookaburras.

6

The spoken word does not belong to this field.
Silence is bread and drink.
I can learn the languages of the air.
Silence is a dream like old inhabitants.
My brother tree & my sister rain invite me
To connect my heart with tranquillity.

Trees

To make
White words on a black page
— Jan Owen

Trees
Unlocked places.
Ink without legal words
To make
White words on a black page.

What am I doing here under these trees
In the middle of this park?
Am I homeless
On a long walk and resting in darkness?
Am I a citizen of long branches
In an open shelter within dry leaves?

The grass is my bed
If I sleep tonight
I will eat the old dream where I find my survival spirit.

A widow on a black canvas

She is in black and smiles a red rose.
She walks as if the wind touches her hips
And balances the air in this urban space.
She is wearing a black long dress.
Her body like autumn leaves falling
Tells where home will be.

Her dark glasses imprison the moon and stars.
My glance frees her tears (and runs through her lips).

She is a widow painted on a black canvas
While I finish this sad poem.

A Morning Blessing

7.05
At the Roma Mitchell Garden
A train is passing and leaves a cloud.
I can see only faces through the windows.
On the other side
We are planting golden nugget pumpkins
In Aunty Maggi's plot.

Hands soil seeds
Straw and water
Elements of life
Together sharing the earth.

Her memory is still growing vegetables in us.

The past is a pelican's wings in the sky
Tribute to her Aboriginal ancestor.

I find a Haiku at Middleton Beach

Wind and waves.
Seagull at Middleton beach
Feet writing in the wet sand.
After a few waves
The afternoon comes
Shore and solitude.
I am reading with pleasure.
The moonlight is my only lamp at sea.

At the West Tent at Writers' Week 2013

The poets read their own poems.

The audience listens to Kurt Heinzelman.
Verses are a unison of words, stanzas and rhythms.

A bird repeats its wild tone to the branch's rhythms.

Up high leaves are spitting water on our faces on this hot day.
Up high a bird is reading its own wild syllables like fruit of the forest.
I saw the poets' panel sitting on the chairs:
Cath Kenneally & Peter Goldsworthy
both look at each other as if a new poem is about to be born.

In the distance I see a poem upon the tree
The audience applauds.
El pájaro the bird
Flies away over the Torrens River.
The poets take all the applause and credit.

Sonnet (Writers' Week in Adelaide, 2006)

I am sitting in different shadows.
Chairs are the roots of trees,
The white tents a nest of words and creation.
I am listening to the sound and face of vowels.
Names and authors are beings of the image world.
Stories of lands, struggles, deaths,
Beauty and ugliness an equal part of the journey.
Foreign sounds are rare birds under the native trees.
A kookaburra sings to the wind and the heat of the evening.
Yahia Al-Samawy reads his poem in Arabic:
Leave my country.
The helmet of occupiers can never be a pigeon's nest.
I am listening to the rhythm of hearts next to a tree.
I am listening to Robert Fisk's flesh,
Wounded lines,
Baghdad and Gaza his home,
Ancient cities without rivers,
Only dried dreams of the oppressors.

Madness systems talking to Michael Dransfield

In the mist
all that is vanishes
—Michael Dransfield

Part one

Un hombre se mira en un espejo
I say darkness echoes *locura.*
Inside the system it gives us food and drink.
I feel, I am looking into a broken mirror & my face is fragments of
    skin & memories,
broken pieces that show me
A wounded man
Sus dedos recorren los bordes del vidrio roto
su piel son alas secas de sangre
I wake up on the ground.
The window has vanished & walls are fallen dreams.
I am a bloody wingless angel eating the fresh verse of the mist.

Part two

Who do you think would live in a house without air. Fish?

Oye vuelve / vuelve con nuestro aire
Hey come back come back with our air.
Here we are breathing too much pollution:
Words, speeches, campaigns
Still invite us
To be part of the politics *de la Locura.*
We are citizens
With a decade of politics
Bombing and fear.
2003, John Howard fridge magnet anti-terrorist package

($15 million the Government spent on the Kit).
2013, Kevin Rudd made the Australian Government's message for
Anyone associated with people smuggling:
IF YOU COME HERE BY BOAT WITHOUT A VISA
YOU WON'T BE
SETTLED IN AUSTRALIA.

I woke up this morning wet
Pieces of dreams were under my bed.
I heard the sea a wild howl in the distance galloping in a big cloud.
It's going to rain all day
It's going to rain all day
It's going to rain
Rain *lluvia*.
How many deaths will there be tonight?

Part three

Don't Brandenburg me
no concerto
No me hago del concierto Brandenburg
concerto no
Por cierto no
concerto no.

Part four

I don't	*No no*
Want to	*quiero quiero*
Freak you out	*asustarte asustarte*
Ian but	*amigo pero amigo pero*
There's someone	*hay alguien hay alguien*
Under the	*debajo*
Bed	*de la cama*
In the system trying	*en el sistema tratando*

Vigilant	*vigilante*
Our soul	*nuestra alma*
To create	*de crear*
A desert	*un desierto*
Where your skin	*donde tu piel*
Be only a dust	*sea polvo*
Easy to shake	*fácil de sacudir*
Already have nothing	*ya no tengas nada que decir ni hacer*
to say or to do	
To change things	*para cambiar las cosas.*

So you decide what to do or how to take courage.
Drink your fear at the bar
And go to bed and read *Monsieur Pain* by Roberto Bolaño
Whoever is under your bed & outside your house.
The tree died last week the birds/*pájaros* fled to exile
While you were sleeping under the system
In front of the TV.
Madness of death and exile.

Part five

In his black magic/house of lords/the men of power/never allowed
You
To be yourself inside the system.
It always will control you.
The system is your air
It will control your mind
And madness *enloquecer* your heart
Beating the rhythm of cruelty under the power of the house of lords
In which we are now & forever. Amen.

Tears

Fall from my heart on those days
It is hurt.
It is ploughed deep into the skin.
It is a *volantin* trapped in an old wire fence
Not as an illusion of blood in a dried river.
In the distance who hears a wounded smile
of a refugee child at Nauru Detention Centre?

Tears fall from my heart on these days.
They flood the land.
Tears fall as wild waves onto the shore.
In the eyes behind the wire
of the security laws of this lucky country.

A poem mirror: within other poets' verses

From being trapped in the point
— *Les Murray*

For a long time I felt
I had been here working & writing
On my blank paper trapped in your consonants
And unable to pronounce or
Breathe the sound of your vowels in the point of your reality.

No-one walks these footpaths. No-one at all
— Graham Rowlands, *The Footpaths*

One night I stayed there. No-one passed next to me.
I was cold and starved.
I walked like a ghost around the rubbish bin.
The street was empty.

I inhabited these footpaths.
If I planted a flag in no-one would land at all.

Ruby loves the smell of earth
— Ali Cobby Eckermann, *Unseen*

I am a survivor of Pinochet's brutal dictatorship.
Ruby was a survivor of the massacre on Ngadjuri land.
Her song is a canto of love to her people
And smells of suffering and courage
And her life is the dream of the earth.

The waiting for the sunrise is like waiting for the past
Of the people to come and proclaim the land
— Lionel Fogarty, *Burn the Bridges*

If we had learned from the past
these generations would make a revolution
but they're waiting for Godot as in the past.
Now, people are watching the sunrise
As a promise to organise the day
And everyone will come from different winds
To proclaim the mother earth free on this occupied land.

We'll all need visas,
For this is the land where hope turns to fear
— John Tranter, *Scenes From a Voyage*

Why do we have to accept a reality like that.
We'll all need visas.
Why don't we stop all wars.
We'll all need visas.
Why aren't we all citizens of the planet earth.
We'll all need visas.
And create a land without borders and police
Where hope becomes a bird
And fear never turns away our poem
To drown the dream of paper boats on the shore of cruelty.

The hunter of verse and flesh

For Geoff Goodfellow

In the Market by 11am
The hunter walks slow and with a sharp glance.

His prey is still a shadow of flesh and passion
Somewhere, in some place, with someone.
The hunter searches without verse or gun.
Time is a body as a river of blood and flesh,
His lips and eyes the only arms in his intimate battle.
He stalks vegetable stalls and meats. He sits at Lucia's table,
Orders a hot chocolate and looks for the next victim or poem.

The hunter is in lilac tie, a flower bud design
Very formal wear for this poet, everything ready for the kill.
He walks towards me; I read a poem in another sound and rhythm.
We shake hands and he confesses the 'hooligan' verse of Esenin's poem:
I am looking for a woman.
The afternoon is strong wind and rain in the city streets wet and cold.

Where is the game of the hunter of bodies.

A short letter to David Hicks

I don't believe what John Howard
Said about you.
I know he was a cynical politician.
The rule of the world is set up by inhuman laws.
Your body wore an orange overall for a sunburnt country.
Chains of death like the jewels of a cruelty system.
Your eyes can only see an instant of life and back to darkness.
In my memory your name is a car sticker: *Free David Hicks*.

Thoughts on a short poem by Les Murray

I hear his language as words on the shore where a patrol boat just left.
I think his verses are at the front of the gate of the old Baxter
   Detention Centre.
I write my own short poem within lively pieces of conversation.
At the long breakfast table
I am reading 'política y Arte' & translating his rhythm.
I feel like one of those asylum seekers
Being sent by a brutal policy to nowhere
Those boats from the deep solitude.
I drink a black coffee at this long table
Where people talk and feast
The sound of politics on my stirring spoon.
I have already read his verse about Brutal Policy
Like rejecting poems and funding them.
Inferior art, said Les, & I write in broken English you know
Les continues: *Whose fault it all is.*

However, I think English is still a colonising tongue
with echoes of white vowels.
Echoes from blood and death in the deep soil of Aboriginal land.

Warrior

To Murray George, Senior Pitjantjatjara Law Man

I saw his
Ancestor presence
Murray George
Senior Pitjantjatjara Law man.
Words, eyes and hands
Are stars, sun and earth
Walking through the NT land.
Illuminating the struggle.
He is amongst his people
A hill of many pathways at his feet
Walking to stop the intervention.

A warrior
Speaking out as a translator of the earth
In the deep accent and rhythm of his heart
As a journey of resistance.
His eyes fresh air to our ill hearts.
Hands and words
Transforming the room into a gum tree
Inviting us to fly or swim
Like a crow or barramundi teaching us
To be in harmony with the law of the Dreamtime.
Eyes and tongue
Speaking English words as a battle
Not as the Coloniser's language
Rather as survival and resistance's warrior.

Eyes looking at us
As a seed of truth during that time
The Intervention's night.

He is a warrior visiting our city
Illuminating the darkness
Of greed and selfishness
Rising up for more than 200 years.

He is a warrior visiting our city
Without an old key to open
This Captain Cook's Paradise.

A Conversation with clouds on the immensity of solitude

They have
Mal dis(ease).
From the middle of nowhere
We travel from Oadlawirra to Wilcannia.
A black crow picks the rest of
Un(ease)
& a wild emu dances with my left hand
Dis(ease).

There is
Deep silence in the plain desert.
I pronounce: drops of rain
As a sound of life.
A dialogue with clouds.

We stop under a
Blue sky and its shadows
Drawing us a border, radio giving us signs of reality.
Make this place a total loss. We break our journey
Distance is a mirror, app(ears) to be
a citizen of death.

Montsalvat Gallery (2010)

East Timor Textiles
Fabric threads of wounds
Colour of pain weaves life and death
As a gift to us.

Earth's colours were cut from the mountains
Resistance dreams of survival
Voices of women like rivers' tears run through
Death's lovers.
Midnight battles (or none)
Sharpen Timor's independence.

Here in Montsalvat after a poetry reading
I carry a bag made by threads of wounds
Of those who lost everything
But the breath to dream and resist
For a new peace
Made by courageous hands and wounded hearts.

Ms Natalie Jean Wood died in Sydney

*No mail piled up. Well before 2003, Ausgrid, formerly Energy Australia, said they sent
some one round to knock on the door before they turned off the power. Sydney Water
said, knowing there was a pensioner at the address, they checked with Centrelink and
were told in 2008 'there was no pensioner there' any longer.*

— *From an article by Janet Fife-Yeomans in* The Advertiser, *July 7, 2011*

Ms Wood, then 79, walked out of the room,
in 2003, to go upstairs to her room where she collapsed and died...

That is how the reporter described her death to us.
An old woman, who died eight years ago alone and nobody missed her.
The neighbour says Ms Wood suffered dementia.

Even the couple who have lived next to her house since 1988
Didn't find any sign of death. Time is muteness and smelliness.
Not even her bones crackle through walls or windows.

I glimpsed her heart and I found dry tears inside an eaten blouse.
Please tell me where is humanity?
Please tell me why the empty street had no eyes and hands?

Didn't anyone knock on the door at Kippax Street, Surry Hills, Sydney,
The place she called home for about 50 years?

I denounce
That as an inhumane crime against a forgotten citizen of Australia.

No mail piled up.
They turned off the power and water.
'There was no pensioner there' any longer.

Ms Wood's skeleton and clothes were eaten by solitude.
The oblivion and air were dark wings in this empty room.
No flowers, coffin or tomb rested in this country.

Only a house forgotten for eight years
In a city of more than 4.5 million citizens.
Ms Wood, it is not a sad poem.
Ms Wood, it is angry and shameful verse.

Streets are overshadowed devoid of humanity.
We live in a time of apathy
Where muteness and coldness grow in our land,
In our streets, and take root in our backyard.

Reading the draft Anti-Terrorism Bill 2005

1
Sometimes a poem is so far from the ink
    An empty page with no words.
Sometimes I embrace the night without a star to pray for.
Sometimes I am naked in front of a dark moon
    and it eats all my flesh and leaves no kiss.
The memory of a dead rose in the blind mirror of your eyes.

2
I saw the news on SBS
The debate on Industrial Relations change & the press conference
By John Howard & Phillip Ruddock
About the Anti-Terrorism laws.
I fell asleep at my desk tired of news,
Tired of searching for poems.

3
After 11.20pm the telephone rang, loudly.
I jumped like a cat feeling the danger of the night.
It was a call from Chile, my sister in law.
She said: I called just to know if you are well.

Coup d'etat

I am a son of an unconstitutional time.
News! News!
What happened to Rudd's economic plan?
More taxes on the mining companies?
Viva Socialism!
Wait a minute, mate.
Coup d' etat and the tax is out.
Julia Gillard is the new PM.

My heart is beating as it was in 1973.
Tanks, soldiers were shadows in empty streets
Within the political crisis.
2010 – Afghanistan or Iraq are lands where
Our soldiers are killing terrorists in 'the name of democracy'.
By the way, back home:
The mining companies save millions in taxes.
They are back to digging, digging.
Reading Judith Wright's
There is no silence on the plains of the Moon
I dug this line into my poem.

Please let him be a bird in this land

To Daggie Sheltens, detainee in Baxter for seven years

The sea is a boat on his dream.
The darkness of the shore embraces
Its journey to a new land.
His visa is only a wave without a name.

Baxter, desert of long sentences
Locked up his youth.
Now his eyes are broken wings.
Now his heart is a cloud in a cage at the detention centre.

He knew where he was in that white room.
He crashed his dream into a native tree in Glenside Hospital.

His mind is a wounded hope for all within the wire desert
Within the white room.

His mind is a bird without air or sky to fly.

Please let him be a bird in this land.

Ng (sound) of the living Ngarrindjeri Nation in this country

We have deprived the natives of their country, sadly diminished
their means of subsistence, and introduced a state of things.
— George Taplin

Sounds of ancient spirits live in this Nation.
Invaders.
Men arrived in 1843, the wind navigating them.
The wildness spoke the Ng stories of everyday.
The consonant flew vaguely and crashed into the old metal of the
   arrivals.
The inhabitants were a combination of roots, waves and wild food.

Ng was a consonant pronouncing the wind, leaves,
Skin of kangaroos for food or clothes inside the wilderness.

Ng had the colour of the moon, the fire of the sun
And the shadows of the naked spirits dancing.

Ng beautiful words build the soul and flesh of the Nation.
Happiness was food to understand life
Before the invaders drummed death
Into the land of the Ngarrindjeri Nation.

Terra Nullius

I live in this terra nullius by Captain Cook
Called Australia
Or perhaps in the *Utopia* by John Pilger
Called Australia.
For sure I am a citizen living in a stolen land
Where their spirit lives for more than 60 000 years.
My verses are made by paper boat.
These poems are refugees on a journey
searching for a place to live.

I am a broken sound
A vowel which I pronounce with the accent of resistance.
I am a political prisoner on Manus Island.

Part 3:
Poems of Struggle & Revolution

Que nadie os haga nunca prisioneros,
Sino es tierra triunfante…
Aconsejada por los limoneros
La libertad un sueño de amapola

— Miguel Hernández

Reading Ernesto Cardenal

Think of those who died,
Of hollows they left in communal graves
Or simply on the ground
Compost for mountain plants.
— Ernesto Cardenal

Birds eat the fruit on the ground
Oscar Romero is yielding aubergines this summer.
Green is the fruit of your saintly life.
For Víctor Jara we planted an acanthus of birds,
water and a yellow heart of melon seeds.

Here lie the prophets, the poets
and all of humanity
who believe in Paradise
growing in communal orchards.

I come from my exile,
my cell closed at the last maize harvest.
I am a starving bird eating leaves and onions.
Here I wait for the tomatoes to kiss the dawn
and reveal the dreams of pigs who were born
on the hot night of the Australian summer.

We are inhabitants of failure,
Allende orphaned us, left us in exile,
lost among bodies that have 'disappeared'
whose names we can never forget.

I read your poems in the light of dictatorship.
Chile back in '78. I fell in love with Claudia, time and again.
I believe fervently
that a Minister for Culture can talk with God
about the plan for the Revolution.

We are verse. I read the master and friend
Ernesto Cardenal from this exile.
From the orchard we plant every day,
from the orchard we harvest every day
at the table where our prayer
becomes bread, nourishment, fruit of the revolution.

The macabre cynical dance (*La danza macabre del cinismo*)

1
Tony Blair

The worst is not, so long as we can say, 'this is the worst'.
— *William Shakespeare, King Lear (Act IV, Scene I)*

Smile through gritted teeth.
A face with white shirt with red tie & power
There's Blair in his dark trade's suit.
Political, speaker of the macabre cynical dance.

There's Gaddafi in the antechamber of treason.

2
Nicolas Sarkozy

One can resist the invasion of an army but one cannot resist the invasion of ideas.
— Victor Hugo

Why didn't Eluard, the French poet, awake Libya?
His verses could be barricades of liberty and resistance.
Sarkozy speaks colonialism's words.
Why are his hands a protocol for death?
There's Gaddafi in the antechamber of treason.

3
Barack Obama

...battles are lost in the same spirit in which they are won.
— Walt Whitman

A face with white shirt with blue tie & power.
Dark suit on his black spirit.
World peace in his hands is a blood product.
Trade figures to invade countries and applaud death.
Leaders smile at the ceremony
Of the macabre cynical dance.

There's Gaddafi in the antechamber of treason.

4
Silvio Berlusconi

Through me the way to eternal pain.
— Dante, Inferno-Hell

Herod on fire in Dante's comedy:
Fire, hell, wine and women in his palace.
A rifle as a gift of death.
Their smile reminds me of the question:
Who will die first?

There's Gaddafi in the antechamber of treason.

How to believe in death?

To Gaddafi and his Green Revolution

How to believe in death
If hatred is a war planned?
It is a distribution of profit and power.
It is nothing else than a financial system in crisis.
NATO-US destroyed homes
With their occupation army of death.
NATO-US made tears like rivers of agony.
NATO-US eyes were open only to desert...

How to believe in death?
Walls fell onto the plates of Palestinian children
Spooned so many tears and bones of the dead.
How to believe in death
If hatred is a legalised document
Of the United Nations General Assembly?
How to believe in death
If power makes dictatorships and disappearances
If power plans massacres and exile
If power plans famine and looting?

How to believe in death
If there was a time I lived in my country happy?
I was a citizen of the streets and a student of hope.
How to believe in death
When Henry Kissinger won the Nobel Peace Prize
In his paradise like shit where he celebrates death?

How to believe in death
When Gaddafi's land was invaded savagely
As the Promised Land for the West?

How to believe in death
If you do not tell us you want our copper,
You want our oil,
You want our salt and our rivers,
You want our land and our mountains,
You want our hearts, our bodies, our minds?

How to believe in life
If you want us as slaves in your 'free world'?
How to believe in death
When I believe the revolution is pregnant
With indigenous ancestors' dreams
and Guevara's spirit on earth, *carajo*!!!

Lenin Taught us to be Free

After State and Revolution, by Vladimir Lenin

Our Father, you were on earth.
Your name: Vladimir Ilyich Lenin.

You gave us the light and the fight.
We taught the *What is to be done?*
You made the revolution
in a few days of class struggle:
      the Soviet Union;
but it fell for Capitalism's temptation.

Bolshevik was your name.
You were an icon for yesterday in 1917,
you gave us our daily bread
in our struggle for
education, bread, work and freedom.

Never forgive those who went to the right
also those who offended you
(Mikhail Gorbachev and all of his traitors.)
We will never forgive them.
Give us new ideas, and more reasons
to commit to our fight
to deliver us from evil Consumerism and Capitalism.

Patria o muerte, Venceremos
as that other apostle on earth, Fidel would say.
Amen.

Reading José Martí

1853
28th January.
La Habana.
A poet was born.
José Martí was his name.
He was a lawyer, poet and a revolutionary,
his land an oppressed colony of Spanish rule;
(he fought in the Independence war)
his land a Casino/*Burdel* for the American marines.
Centuries of underground struggles.

Martí was 17 years old after he lived a century
volver a los 17, después de vivir un siglo, como decía Violeta.
Cuba was a forest of freedom's thoughts.
Trees were long poems of liberty and dreams
grown to defend the heart of the father of Independence in Cuba.
Martí in exile in New York
learned to know early the birth of Capitalism from inside.
His verses of struggle have been read for more than
a century.
Cuba is a revolution
Of 50 years of blockade by the US.

Martí, padre, poeta y revolucionario.
Cuba, Fidel and Che were disciples, Martiriano.
José Martí,
Padre, poeta y revolucionario.
Tierra donde la libertad y sus hijos pobres
son, sol y salsa's rhythm
shared dreams of freedom.
I am reading his Simple verses

in this Kaurna land
of 60,000 years of Aboriginal inheritance,
but they are the poorest inhabitants of Australia.
José Martí, 157 years old.
Prison and exile *prisión y exilio*
were poems and politics
embracing dreams of a new liberation
of Latin-American people.
As he said:
With the poor of this earth
I would like to share my fate.
Con los pobres de la tierra
quiero yo mi suerte echar.

From the North, at five in the afternoon

After Federico García Lorca's 'Lament for Ignacio Sánchez Mejías

The dawn is full of darkness
The whole day has roots of broken wings in the sky.
Five faces and hearts are courageous.
Five names in the revolution are brave against the north.

Men are warriors for freedom.
Men are fathers, sons, and husbands
And lovers of the revolution.
Five suns with rays, eyes
And consciences for humanity.

Their hearts beating towards the South,
Knowing the North is preparing
Rivers of blood for other lands.
Their hearts beating towards the South
Knowing the North is preparing
More clouds of invasion
With steel bullets of liars.

Men are waves of dignity
Tracking the evil system.
Bells of freedom resound around the world
For these five warriors of freedom,
At five in the afternoon.

Cuba Sí

Es tierno lo que nace es tierna Cuba
Es decir que te ofrezco todos mis nacimientos
— *Juan Gelman*

Is another world possible?
Yes!!

We landed in José Martí Airport.
A dream in our fist
in our blood
in our eyes
comes through
the air, the sky and the verses of the fatherhood's poet.
The language we speak there
has the daily syllables and sounds of *Revolución.*

Words and things speak to us:
an old (Soviet) tractor carries people to work or home;
and as well another old (Soviet) tractor carries onions in Banao's town.
'8 hours of blockade is equal to materials to repair
40 School Care Centres.'

To travel in Cuba:
guaguas, cars, *camellos*, bici-taxi, the driver and passengers
not knowing each other.
However, they have a common destiny
Within the roads of *Revolución.*

Radio Rebelde, we hear from this...
'If you have a problem with your mates
say something to them,
start a new day with a smile in your heart.'

Organipónico, a community garden,
everywhere in each town,
on the highway or on small pieces of land:
vegetables are fresh for the table of the *Revolución.*

A machete to cut *cortar*
A machete to prune *podar*
A machete in black hands put an end to slavery.
Today those hands cut the *amapolas* and red bougainvilleas.
The pathway to Granma, 1800 metres from the ocean.
Small ships within waves of *Revolución.*
Granma arose fifty years ago
weed and *fango* the invincible giants of tyranny.
Ocean, weed and *fango* imprison hearts in this journey,
Fidel a prophet, *El Comandante,*
crossed the ocean into the immensity of tyranny.
A *revolución* began in deep water,
fango and high, long weeds of nothingness.

Somos nosotros los habitantes de la noche,
la llevamos como sombras heredadas.
El cuerpo del padre en nosotros
cortado entre el sueño y la revolución.

Between two rivers the poet fell;
his death the seeds of bosque Martiano
where trees —
Ceiba, Yaya, Palma, Guacima, Jupiter, Periquillo, Acansa, Algarrobo —
give branches to birds and winds
dentro de la corteza el verso.
There are inhabitants where *La Revolución* grows day by day
hay ciudadanos de donde la revolución crece día a día.
A banner in the street of Bayamo town:
Con Fidel Presente
Con Raul al frente
Venceremos.

The key of my house

For thousands of Palestinian people
Home doesn't exist anymore.
Why?
Home and this key have equal memories.
You can go in and stay there
Eating, talking and laughing
Sleeping with your children and family.
Not in Palestine.
Why?
The key opens not only the door.
It is where you live and where your roots come from.
The key is not only a piece of metal; the key opens life to
Love and happiness.
The key is not a symbol; it is part of your life.
The key is given to you in trust and care
So why take away my home and leave me the key?
I open my memories, my heart, and through my eyes
Tears fall like earthquakes or bombs in my soul.
I don't know what to do.
Without a land, without a home only this key is evidence.
I am Palestinian and I grew up and live here in this holy land

The Ruined City

Winter rain washed blood
from streetlights into gutters
— *Chris Abani*

I feel as if I am a ruined city
where occupying soldiers
destroy myself as well as my home
schools, churches
playgrounds, markets
government buildings, universities…everything.

I feel as if I am a ruined city
where occupying soldiers
shoot bodies
within thousands of children's eyes.

I feel as if I am a ruined city
where occupying soldiers
do not touch an old mother
washing her family's clothes
dirtied not by playing or mucking about
but by death, death, death.

The moon is howling somewhere
rubble, rubble in innocent blood.

I must rebuild my home in my heart.
That is the only way to reclaim my city
GAZA.

The Market vs God

The Vatican said it had ended 2009
With a loss of €4.1 million (A$5.93 million) AFP

Oh modern creation.
Species depend on it.
Money is the seed on earth,
The heart of existence.
Without it, what can we do?
Nothing.

Corporations have expelled God
And Darwin enough
Not from the deepwater oil spill on the US shore
Where thousands of sea-species are in torment.
Not prayers or lament
Can give salvation to mother earth.

We live for money:
We prefer to call ourselves consumers & customers
Rather than individuals.
Paradise now is only a biblical term.

According to the shopping centre advertisement
The shopping list is our daily prayer.
We can go to heaven if we win a free drink,
Coke, the blessed drink on earth
fish & chips our daily bread.

The Market's spirit is amongst us.
Nietzsche said God is dead.
Do we remain all alone now in the world?

Where is humanity in this financial crisis?
The Market eats the soul & self.

The King's Speech

To Fidel Castro, prophet and comrade of our time

I went back less than a hundred years
When I saw the movie *The King's Speech*
at the same time I received the last
reflections by Comrade Fidel on Obama's speech in Arizona.

What an amazing parallel for a poem.
Sitting in my hands, with all material
and taste, it is a great piece of writing.
We live in a time where we all stammer like a plague since we were
    born.
Whatever we say the powerful can't hear us.
We can rewind or go forward
into the reality as if we have in our hand the remote control.
However a long list of atrocities, pain, war, death,
colonisation are the facts of daily bread.
Unfortunately for millions of people this bread
is not blessed or holy at all.

Fidel plays for me in our world
the role of the speech therapist, Lionel Logue.
His reflections are the true water for our thirsty mind
in a world where everything is controlled by the big Corporations of
    Media
that make us slaves of the mind and only exist on one side of the moon.
He can think deeply through the water of reality.

King George VI, he couldn't pronounce a single word
in one of his speeches just before he announced
the World War years of 1939-1945.
The speech therapist helped him to be able to speak to the whole Empire
And he finished with a poem:
I said to the man who
stood at the Gate of the Year,
Give me a light that
I may tread safely into the unknown.
But Fidel said to Obama: *What transforms a president*
into a historical personage, who has been able to reach that position
because of his merits, does not lie in the person. But in the need for him
at a determinate moment in the history of his nation.

As in the speech therapy of King George VI,
Fidel gave us a deep understanding
of the US Presidency and its historical moment.
Again and again the question: To be or not to be,
and its quest…wait for a human answer on the atrocities of killing,
the ashes of war, the inhuman political blockade against Cuba,
the military coups everywhere.
Death
hunger
natural disasters happening on our planet, today.
That is why Fidel on reflection said of Mr Obama
… *for a political speech, left a lot to be desired.*

In this modern Time

The sacred ambitions of the system
Hold to ransom the souls of countries.
Abundant the fruits of the earth
As the years turn through
Political and military intervention.
Poverty becomes a currency negotiable
By instalments paid over a thousand years.
In this modern Time
The minerals of transnational ambitions,
The black gold of power,
Rubbish dumped in the waters of the oceans,
The pollution of southern lakes,
The indiscriminate felling of native forests
Represent the civilization of capital and legacy
Of Western culture.

What is this? More liberty given to the free market?
Less social justice to the people?
Money is more important
Than regard for human rights.
In this modern Time
Political silence in international places
Is a political vote for new economic loans.

In this modern Time
A country's priority is to improve its image of political stability
To provide the best welcome for the sacred investment bank.
What is the price of politics mixed up with so much corruption?
The answer is sacred: capital gains.
The rubbish in the streets is nothing compared
With the genocide of the poor
Who survive in the social margins of the free market system.

In real life
Even though a light heart drives away trouble,
The victims will never have an international treaty.

Learn how to make a Revolution

It would be a mistake to imagine that the people's revolutionary movement in Egypt theoretically obeys a reaction to violations of their most elementary rights. Peoples do not defy repression and death, nor do they remain for nights on end protesting energetically, just because of merely formal matters. They do this when their legal and material rights are being mercilessly sacrificed to the insatiable demands of corrupt politicians and the national and international circles looting the country.

— Fidel Castro, Reflections on the Revolutionary Rebellion in Egypt

Long live the Egyptian Revolution!
When was the last time you heard about a revolution?
It is born from the cry of the people.
The revolution is possible.
We have to believe in it.
This is when the voices are loud and march in the street.
We are too afraid to call a revolution
to hold our fists and shoes up in the air.
Voices in the streets of oppression
build a camp of dreams to change and defy tyranny
to create many liberation squares around the country as meeting places
where we recognise each other's faces and sorrows.

You, a person with your strength and weakness
stand as tree metal or bridge to defend
the dignity of the nation.
People's hearts are united like a flock of courageous birds
all together flying in one direction through the sky.

You clean, sweep your streets
to rebuild paradise from fire and corruption.
Your rebellion
your revolution
your eighteen days of rebellion
days and nights on the streets
as barricades of hope, justice and human sacrifices
your eighteen days against the tyrant.
Abajo Hosni Mubarak! Fuera, fuera!
Down with Hosni Mubarak! Out, out the Dictator!

The Egyptian revolution is a seed of unity, courage
planted in your land.
Walls are the people's newspaper in Gaza.
All its citizens read and celebrate
on their apartheid's wall the Egyptian revolution.

Notes

'Go to be lost to others, overwhelmed/ by bones and light and themselves' takes its title from 'The Merry-Go-Round by the Sea' by John Kinsella, from the book *Armour*

'A rose bush blossomed as a poet died' was translated by Peter Boyle

'Conversation with Yahia Al-Samawy' uses some lines from Yahia Al-Samawy's poem 'A Tombstone from the Marble of Words'

'Summer's morning about 11am' refers to a dog called Rex, who lives in our community garden

'Cultural Difference' refers to drinking 'mate', which is a traditional herbal drink in South America

'Madness systems talking to Michael Dransfield' uses some lines from the poem 'Madness Systems', by Michael Dransfield.

'Ms Natalie Jean Wood died in Sydney' is based upon an article written by Janet Fife-Yeomans in *The Advertiser* on July 7, 2011

'Reading Ernesto Cardenal' was translated by Ana María Crowe Serrano

'Lenin Taught us to be Free' was inspired by *State and Revolution*, by Vladamir Lenin, Chapter 2, page 45

'From the North, at five in the afternoon' takes its title from Federico García Lorca's poem, 'Lament for Ignacio Sánchez Mejías'

'Learn how to make a revolution' was inspired by an article by Fidel Castro published in *Granma* magazine on February 13, 2011, 'Reflections on the Revolutionary Rebellion in Egypt'

Acknowledgments

Poems from this collection have appeared in the following publications:

'Talking with Nicanor Parra in Santiago in 1981': *The Turnrow Anthology of Contemporary Australian Poetry*, John Kinsella, ed. Turnrow Books, 2014

'Please let him be a bird in this land': *The Turnrow Anthology of Contemporary Australian Poetry*, John Kinsella, ed. Turnrow Books, 2014

'Please let him be a bird in this land': Singer/songwriter Jen Lush has included the poem 'Please Let Him Be a Bird in this land' in her poetry-music project, along with 11 other Australian poems made into songs for a cd release in 2016

'Red Chilli': *The Turnrow Anthology of Contemporary Australian Poetry*, John Kinsella, ed. Turnrow Books, 2014

'Monday 12 July at 2 pm': *Overland*, issue 203, winter, 2011, p. 72

'Javier Chavez's Sunflowers': *Revista de Poesía Pata de Liebre* by Aristóteles España. Chile 2007

'Go to be lost to others, overwhelmed/ by bones and light and themselves': The Disappearing; The Red Room Company Project 2012, & on Radio National on The Disappearing, Saturday 1 February, 2014, 3:05PM

'A Conversation with Clouds on the immensity of solitude': DIS(EASE), UN(EASE), MIS(EASE), APP(EASE) Anything But Human by Julie Clarke & Wednesday, July 31, 2013

'Reading Ernesto Cardenal': *Shadowtrain* (UK: Issue 10, November 2006) Translation copyright @ Anamaria Crowe Serrano, 2006

'The King's Speech': *Adelaide Voices Community Newspaper,* March/May 2011

'In this modern Time': *Adelaide Voices Community Newspaper,* Feb/March 1995

'Sonnet (Writers' Week in Adelaide, 2006)': *Famous Reporter # 33,* July 2006

'Playing chess against a maldita white queen', 'The war remains far away', 'Thoughts on a short poem by Les Murray', 'Please let him be a bird in this land', 'Terra Nullius', and 'Reading Ernesto Cardenal': *The Ukrainian Literary Newspaper,* April/May 2020. Translated into Ukranian by Svetlana Lavochkina

Acknowledgments and Gratitude

Thanks to Graham Rowlands and Christine Ingleton for providing editorial advice; to Mike Ladd and Radio National's Poetica; Red Room Company; Radio Adelaide's Breakfast Art Show; Radio Adelaide's Wide Open Road 'I Citizen'; Tony Collins & Carmel Young. Thanks to Steve Brock and Sergio Holas for reading the manuscript.

A deep thanks to my friend Michele Seminara and to Ross Gillett, David Musgrave and Morgan Arnett for their wonderful final editing and comments on my manuscript.

Thanks to the poet and friend, Svetlana Lavochkina, from Ukrainian/German for translating into Ukrainian language six of my poems belonging to this book.

www.ingramcontent.com/pod-product-compliance
Lightning Source LLC
Chambersburg PA
CBHW030843090426
42737CB00009B/1092